Countries of the World

Nicaragua

by Janet Riehecky

Consultant:
Thomas W. Walker, Ph.D.
Director of Latin American Studies
Ohio University

Bridgestone Books
an imprint of Capstone Press
Mankato, Minnesota

Bridgestone Books are published by Capstone Press
151 Good Counsel Drive, P.O. Box 669, Mankato, Minnesota 56002
http://www.capstone-press.com

Library of Congress Cataloging-in-Publication Data
Riehecky, Janet, 1953–
     Nicaragua/by Janet Riehecky.
     p. cm.—(Countries of the world)
     Includes bibliographical references (p. 24) and index.
     Summary: Introduces the geography, animals, food, and culture of Nicaragua.
     ISBN 0-7368-1107-9
     1. Nicaragua—Juvenile literature. [1. Nicaragua.] I. Title. II. Countries of the world
(Mankato, Minn.)
F1523.2 .R54 2002
972.85—dc21

                                                                            2001003431

Editorial Credits
Rebecca Glaser, editor; Karen Risch, product planning editor; Linda Clavel, cover production
     designer; Erin Scott/SARIN Creative, illustrator; Alta Schaffer, photo researcher

Photo Credits
Audrius Tomonis/www.banknotes.com, 5 (bottom right)
Chip and Rosa Maria Peterson, 6, 8
Cory Langley, cover, 10, 12, 14, 18, 20
Flag Folio, 5 (top left)
Joe McDonald, 16

1 2 3 4 5 6 07 06 05 04 03 02

Table of Contents

Official Name: Republic of Nicaragua
Capital: Managua
Population: About 5 million
Language: Spanish
Religions: Roman Catholic, Protestant

Size: 49,998 square miles
(129,495 square kilometers)
Nicaragua is a little larger than the U.S. state of New York.
Crops: coffee, bananas, sugar, cotton

Maps

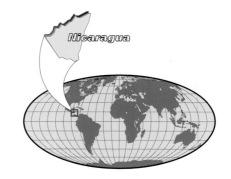

Flag

The flag of Nicaragua has three stripes with the country's coat of arms in the center. The blue stripes show that the country is bordered by water on two sides. The white stripe stands for purity. The words "Republica de Nicaragua America Central" form a circle around the coat of arms. The blue triangle shows a sea, five volcanoes, a red cap, and a rainbow. This flag was adopted on August 27, 1971.

Currency

The unit of currency in Nicaragua is the gold cordoba. One hundred centavos make up one gold cordoba.

In the early 2000s, about 13 gold cordobas equaled 1 U.S. dollar. About 8 gold cordobas equaled 1 Canadian dollar.

The Land

Nicaragua is the largest country in Central America. Honduras borders Nicaragua to the north. Costa Rica lies to the south. On the west coast is the Pacific Ocean. On the east coast is the Caribbean Sea.

Nicaragua has many types of land and water. Rich farmland lies along the Pacific coast. A row of volcanoes stands farther inland. Lake Nicaragua and Lake Managua are two large freshwater lakes in Nicaragua. Rolling hills and mountains cover the central part of the country. The east coast has rain forests, grasslands, and swamps. No good roads connect the east coast to the west coast. These two areas seem like separate countries.

Nicaragua lies slightly north of the equator. The weather usually is hot and humid. The average temperature is 87 degrees Fahrenheit (31 degrees Celsius). It is cooler in the mountains. Nicaragua has a wet season from July to October. The dry season lasts for the rest of the year.

This volcano is near the city of Leon.

Life at Home

Nicaragua is a poor country. Most families need at least two people working so they can afford food, clothing, and shelter.

In the countryside, many homes lack electricity or running water. These homes often are made from wood, plastic bags, or mud bricks. Almost half of Nicaraguans work on farms. They may be able to work only during harvest time.

In cities, conditions are a little better. Some people are rich. They live in large homes with many servants. But many Nicaraguans live in poor, crowded neighborhoods called barrios (BAR-ee-ohz). Many people do not have cars or telephones. Most people have a radio. Children sometimes work to earn money for their family. They may sell items such as newspapers in the streets.

Nicaraguan families are large. Many families have five or six children. Grandparents, uncles, aunts, and cousins often live near family members.

Nicaraguan families often are large.

Disasters

Earthquakes, volcanic eruptions, tsunamis, and hurricanes have damaged Nicaragua. One of the strongest earthquakes destroyed the capital city of Managua in December 1972. About 20,000 people died. Much of the damage never has been fixed.

In April 1992, a volcano named Cerro Negro erupted twice in one week. Volcanic ash covered the ground as far as 15 miles (24 kilometers) southwest of the volcano. It destroyed crops, livestock, and thousands of homes. Cerro Negro also erupted in 1995 and 1999.

In September 1992, an earthquake off Nicaragua's west coast caused a tsunami. This large sea wave destroyed thousands of homes.

On October 30, 1998, Hurricane Mitch struck Nicaragua. High winds caused more than $1 billion in damage. Heavy rains created huge mudslides and floods. Thousands of people died.

This Managua building was damaged in an earthquake.

Going to School

Before 1980, more than half of Nicaraguans could not read or write. In the 1980s, the government built schools and sent volunteers to teach. After that, only 13 percent could not read. Since 1990, the government has not helped schools as much. Today, about 23 percent of Nicaraguans cannot read and write.

About three-fourths of Nicaraguan children ages 6 to 13 go to primary school. Children often work to help support their family. Less than half of primary school children go on to secondary school.

Schools in Nicaragua are crowded. Many schools have two five-hour shifts per day. Students attend school in either the morning or afternoon.

Nicaraguan students learn to read, write, and do arithmetic. They may also study how to plant and care for crops. Many schools close during harvest time. The children help bring in the crops. Students also do chores at their school.

Students in Nicaragua wear school uniforms.

Nicaraguan Food

Most meals in Nicaragua include rice and beans. Gallo pinto (GUY-oh PEEN-toh) is a popular rice and bean dish. People fry red beans, rice, onions, garlic, and spices in hot oil to make it. Many Nicaraguans like spicy food. They add a spicy sauce called salsa to almost everything they eat.

The corn tortilla (tor-TEE-yuh) is a popular food in Nicaragua. Tortillas are flat, round bread. Nicaraguans fill tortillas with beans or meats. Tamales (tuh-MAHL-eez) are tortillas made with corn, cheese, and hot peppers.

Bananas are an important crop in Nicaragua. Nicaraguans like to eat them plain. They also make cakes, porridge, and milk shakes from bananas.

Coffee beans are another important crop. Nicaraguans drink coffee all day. They often add a little milk to it in the morning. They drink coffee with lots of sugar added the rest of the day.

Gallo pinto is a popular rice and bean dish.

Animals

Many kinds of animals live in Nicaragua. Deer and coyotes live in Nicaragua's grasslands. Parrots, macaws, and toucans live in Nicaragua's rain forests. Monkeys, pumas, and jaguars also are found in the rain forests.

Nicaragua's large lakes and bordering oceans are home to many marine animals. Many freshwater and saltwater fish live there. Turtles, manatees, snakes, alligators, and crocodiles also make their home in Nicaragua's waters. Dolphins and whales can be seen off the coast. Lake Nicaragua is home to the only freshwater sharks in the world.

Many of Nicaragua's lakes are polluted. Waters become polluted when harmful materials flow into lakes and rivers. Pollution can harm marine life. Animals such as the largetooth sawfish and the hawksbill turtle may become extinct. Nicaragua is working to keep these and other animals from dying out.

Jaguars roam Nicaragua's rain forests.

Sports and Games

Baseball is the most popular sport in Nicaragua. Fans follow their local teams. They also follow the major league teams in the United States and Canada.

In Nicaragua, more than 200 baseball teams play at local or national levels. Most cities have their own baseball stadium. Children play baseball in empty lots on weekends and holidays. They may use a stick for a bat and a rock wrapped in rags for a ball.

Nicaraguans enjoy other sports such as boxing and soccer. Volleyball and basketball also are popular.

Bull fighting also draws large crowds. In Spain and other countries, the matador tries to kill the bull. In Nicaragua, the matador must try to get onto the bull and ride it.

Many young people play baseball in Nicaragua.

Holidays and Celebrations

September 15 is Nicaragua's Independence Day. The country declared independence from Spain on this day in 1821. People celebrate with parades, fireworks, music, and speeches. Nicaraguans also celebrate July 19. On this day in 1979, they overthrew Anastasio Somoza. He was a cruel dictator whose family had ruled the country for 42 years.

Most people in Nicaragua practice Christianity. This religion follows the teachings of Jesus Christ. Christian holidays such as Easter and Christmas are very important to Nicaraguans.

In early December, Christians celebrate La Purisma. This festival honors the Virgin Mary, mother of Jesus Christ. This holiday began hundreds of years ago. A volcano had been erupting for days. The eruption stopped after a statue of Mary was placed by the volcano. The people believed Mary stopped it. Today, many families put up altars to Mary in their homes. They sing songs and pray.

Girls sometimes wear traditional dresses for Independence Day celebrations.

Hands On: Paint a Mural

Nicaragua sometimes is called the "world capital of mural art." Murals are large paintings on walls that often tell a story. Nicaragua has many murals. Some of the murals tell about Nicaragua's history.

What You Need

Several people
Large roll of white paper
Pencils
Paint
Paint brushes
Cleaning rags
Masking tape

What You Do

1. Choose a story to show on the mural. You could show the history of your school or a story about a recent event where you live.
2. Roll out the paper on the floor.
3. Have different people draw each part of the story in pencil. The parts of the story should be in order.
4. Paint the drawings. Clean up the paints and brushes when you are done.
5. Use the masking tape to hang your mural on a wall.

Learn to Speak Spanish

Most of the people of Nicaragua speak Spanish, which uses the same alphabet as English.

hello	hola	(OH-lah)
goodbye	adiós	(ah-dee-OHS)
yes	sí	(SEE)
no	no	(NOH)
please	por favor	(POR fah-VOR)
thank you	gracias	(GRAH-see-ahs)
mother	madre	(MAH-drey)
father	padre	(PAH-drey)

Words to Know

dictator (DIK-tay-tur)—a person who has complete power to rule over a country

equator (ee-KWAY-tur)—an imaginary line around the earth; the equator is halfway between the north and south poles.

extinct (ek-STINGKT)—no longer living anywhere in the world

humid (HYOO-mid)—damp and moist

marine (muh-REEN)—having to do with the ocean or sea

matador (MAT-uh-dor)—a bullfighter

purity (PYOOR-ih-tee)—being free from evil

salsa (SAHL-suh)—a spicy sauce usually made from tomatoes, hot peppers, and onions

Read More

Griffiths, John. *Nicaragua.* Major World Nations. Philadelphia: Chelsea House, 1999.

Morrison, Marion. *Nicaragua.* Enchantment of the World. New York: Children's Press, 2001.

Useful Addresses and Internet Sites

Consulado General de Nicaragua en Montreal
4870 Doherty
Montreal, Quebec H4V 2B2
Canada

Embassy of Nicaragua
1627 New Hampshire Avenue NW
Washington, D.C. 20009

CIA World Factbook—Nicaragua
http://www.odci.gov/cia/publications/factbook/geos/nu.html
Experience Nicaragua—Culture
http://library.thinkquest.org/17749/culture.html?tqskip=1

Index